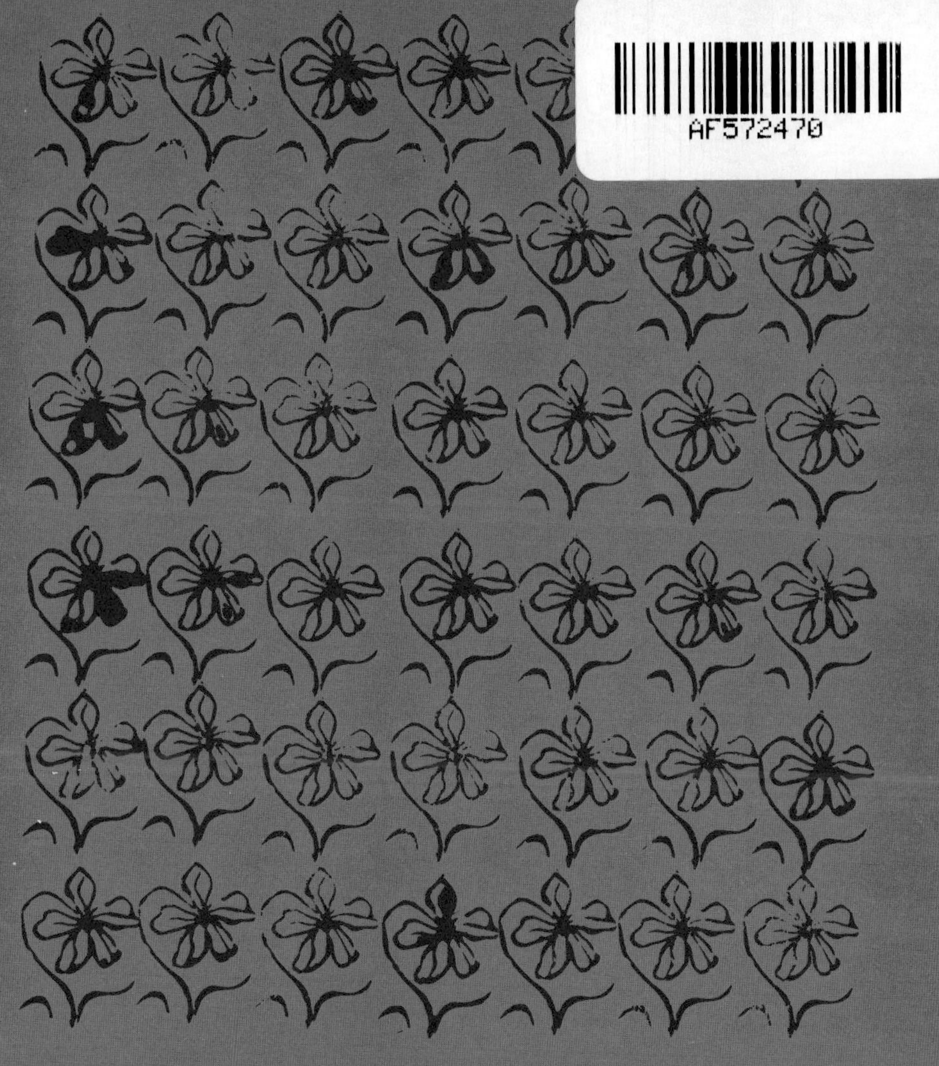

FLOWERS, FLOWERS, FLOWERS

FLOWERS, FLOWERS, FLOWERS

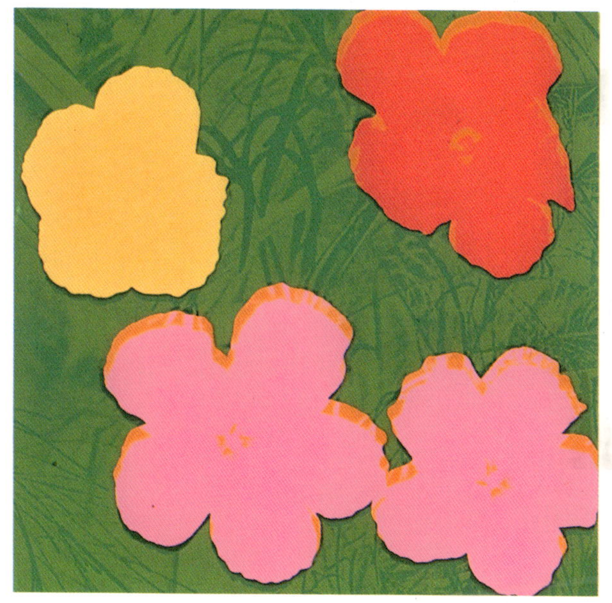

ANDY WARHOL

A BULFINCH PRESS BOOK

LITTLE, BROWN AND COMPANY BOSTON NEW YORK TORONTO LONDON

FIRST EDITION
Quotations from Andy Warhol compiled by R. Seth Bright
Designed by John Kane

Library of Congress Cataloging-in-Publication Data

Warhol, Andy, 1928–1987.
Flowers, flowers, flowers / Andy Warhol. — 1st ed.
p. cm.
"A Bulfinch Press Book"
Includes bibliographical references.
ISBN 0-8212-2289-9 (hc)
1. Warhol, Andy, 1928–1987 — Themes, motives. 2. Flowers in art.
I. Title.
NC139.W37A4 1996
760'.092 — dc20 95-46283

Bulfinch Press is an imprint and trademark of
Little, Brown and Company (Inc.)
Published simultaneously in Canada by
Little, Brown & Company (Canada) Limited

PRINTED IN SINGAPORE

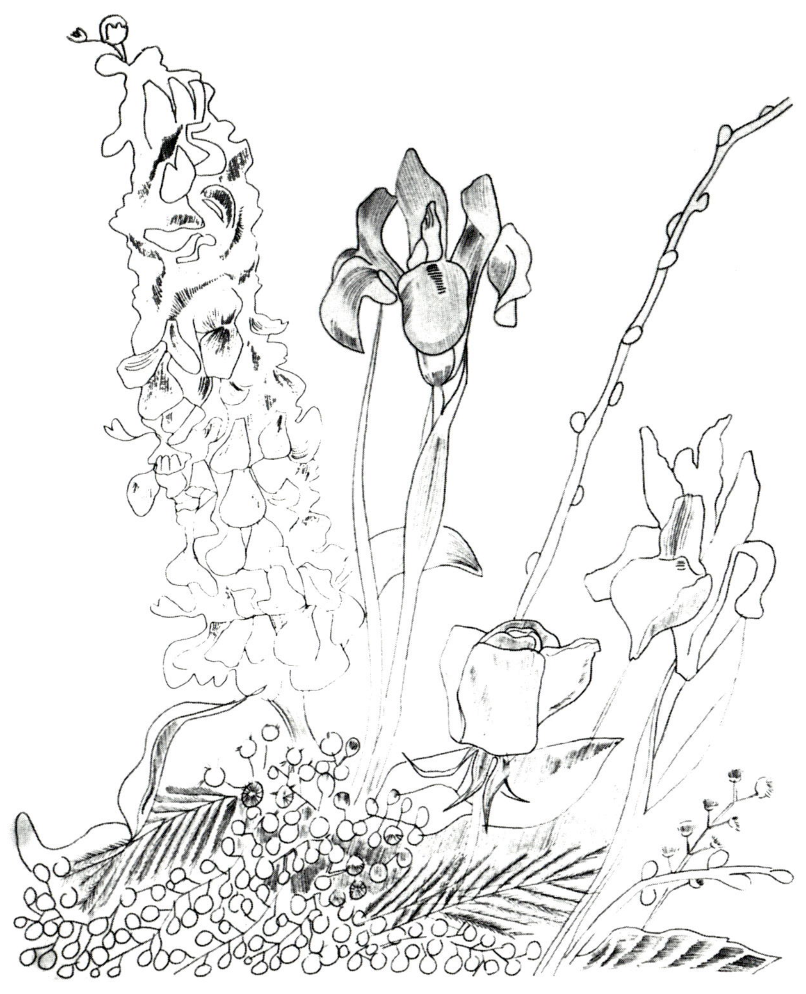

I would have filmed

a flower

giving birth

to another

flower.

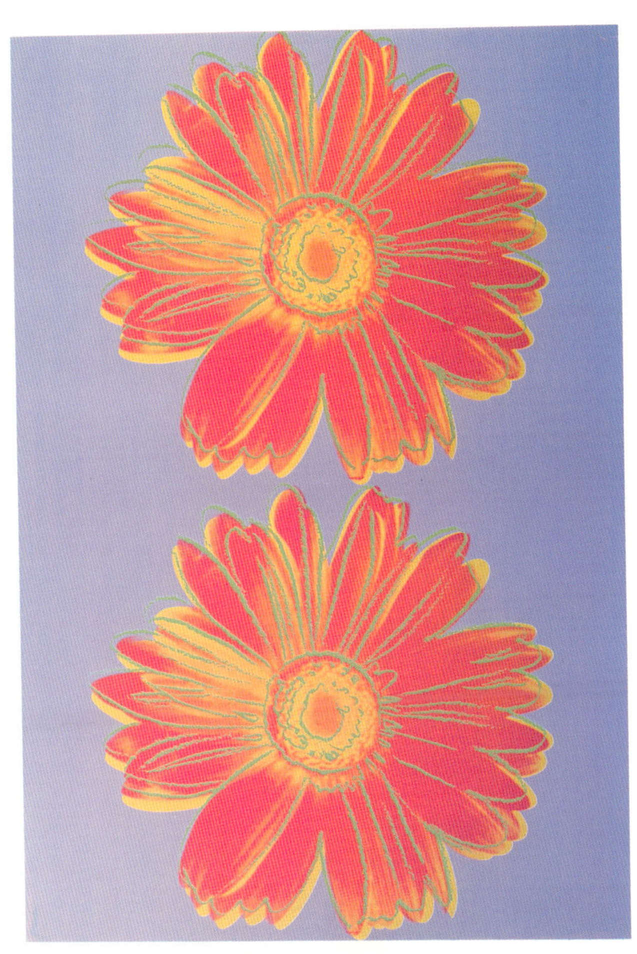

Then you bring those home
and your room is

filled with
flowers.

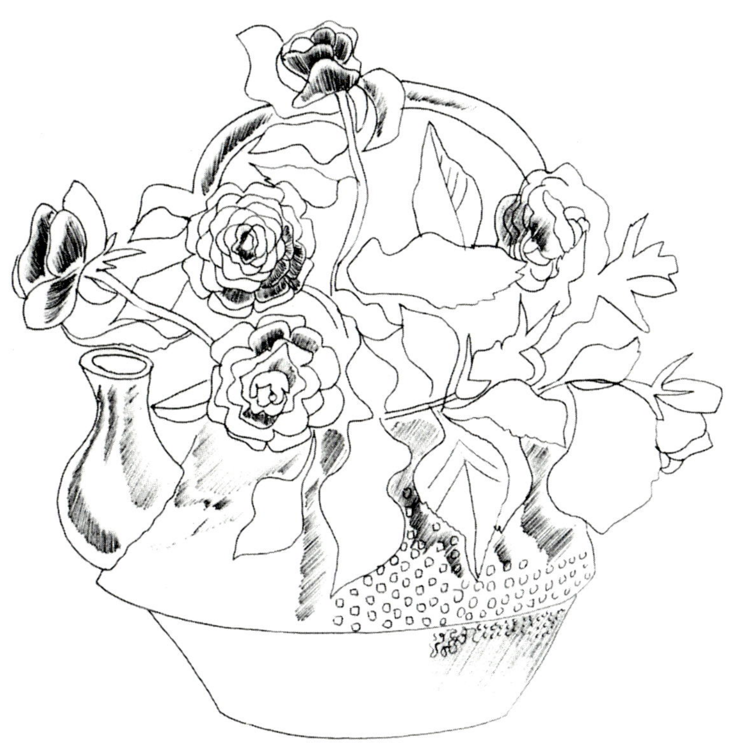

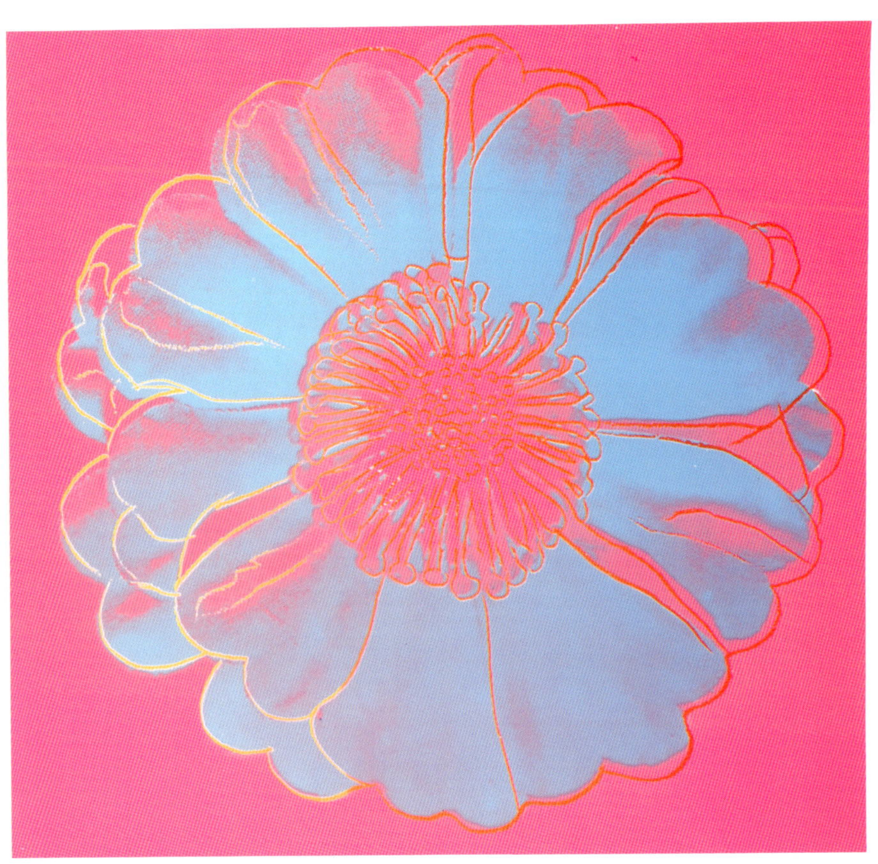

They put out a **mood**
that makes them
more beautiful.

Some people I know
spend **a lot** of time
trying to dream up
new seductions.

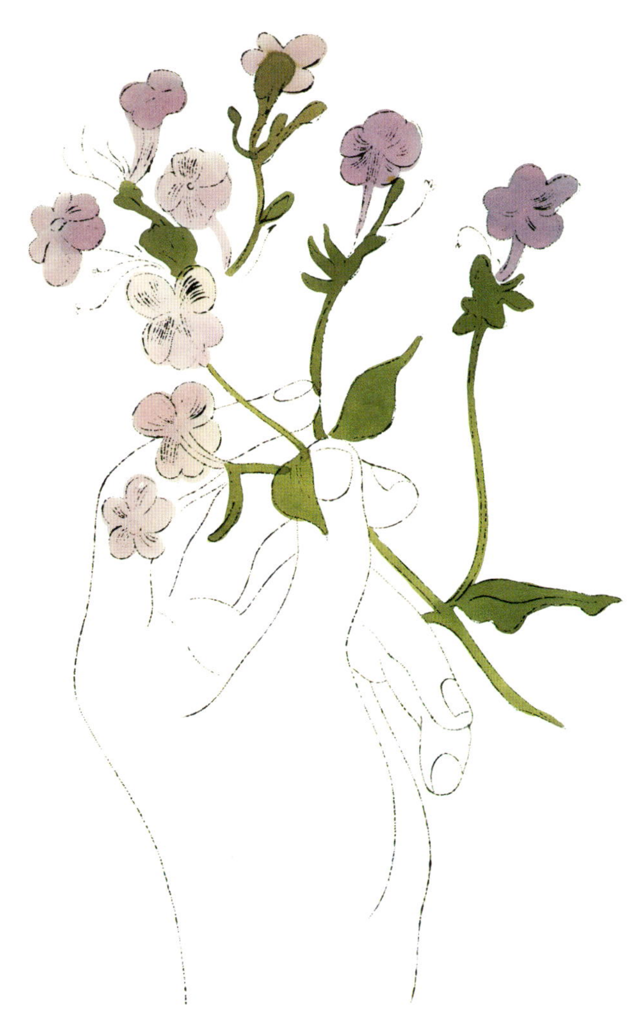

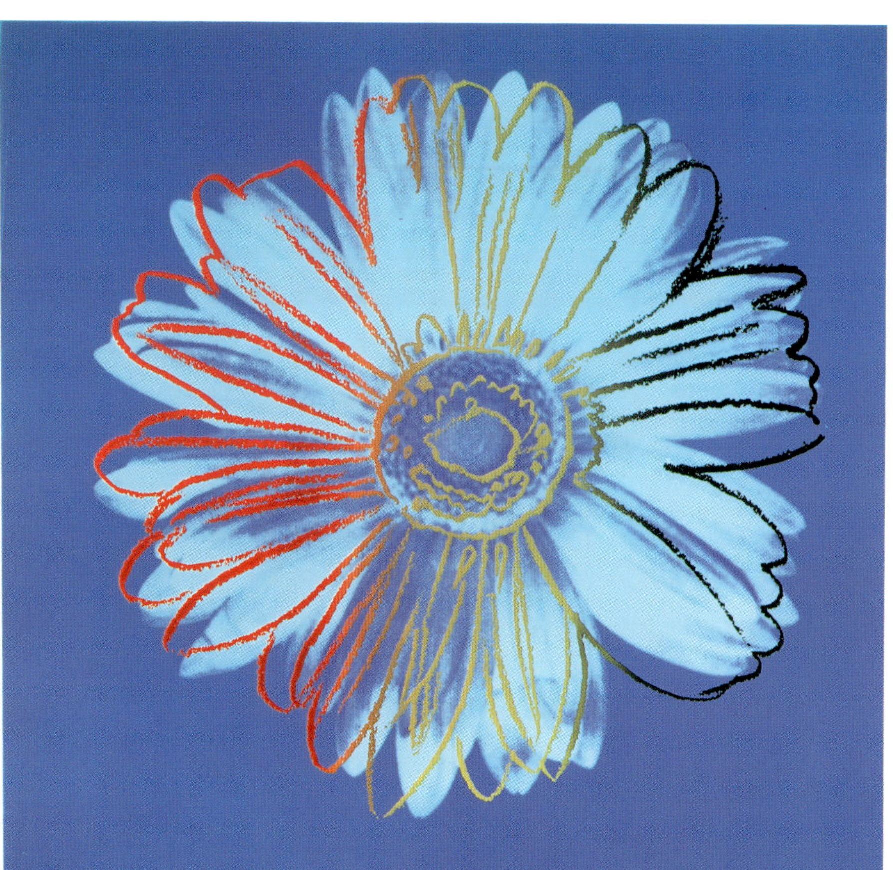

All in all,

it looks like

the **perfect**

setting.

You can really get a **good look**

at the **flowers**

before the **crush** starts.

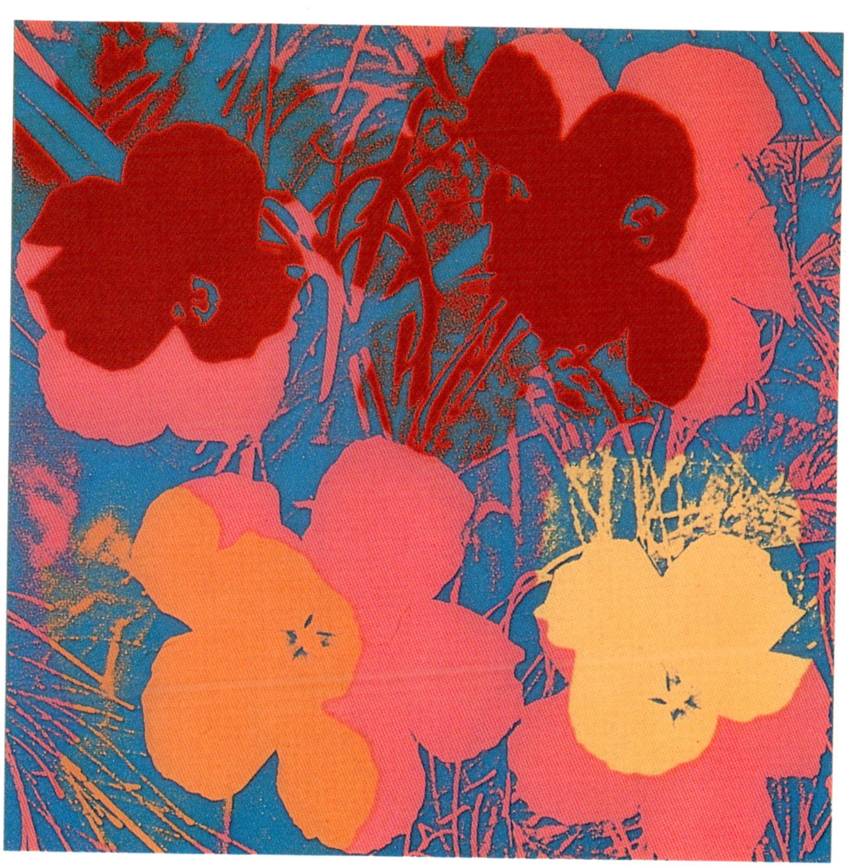

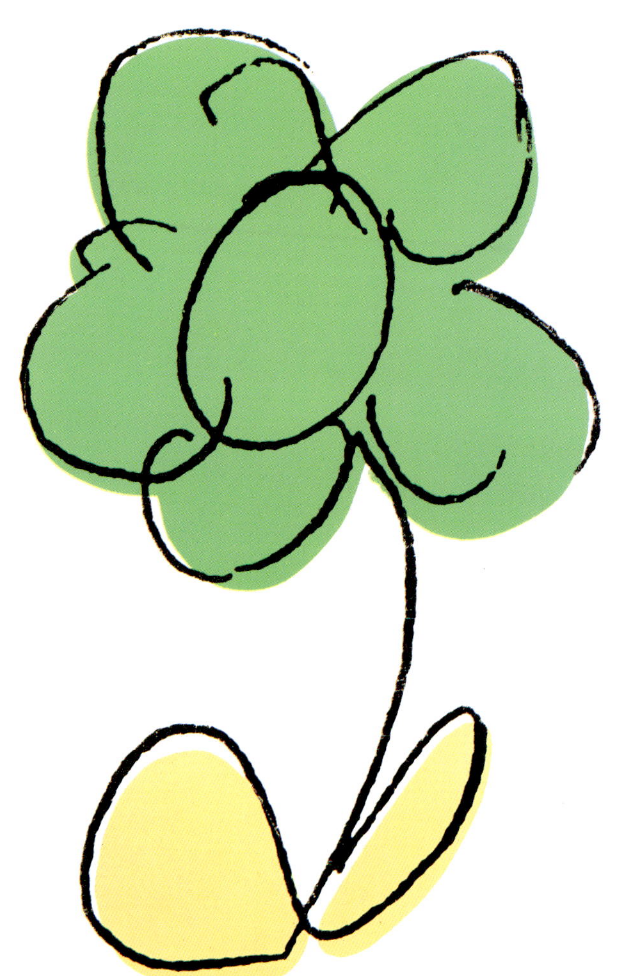

When you have flowers
at home,
you should have
someone
come to the house.

Sometimes I picture
a botany book in the future
saying something like, "The lilac
is now extinct.
Its fragrance is thought
to have been similar
to—?" and then what can they say?

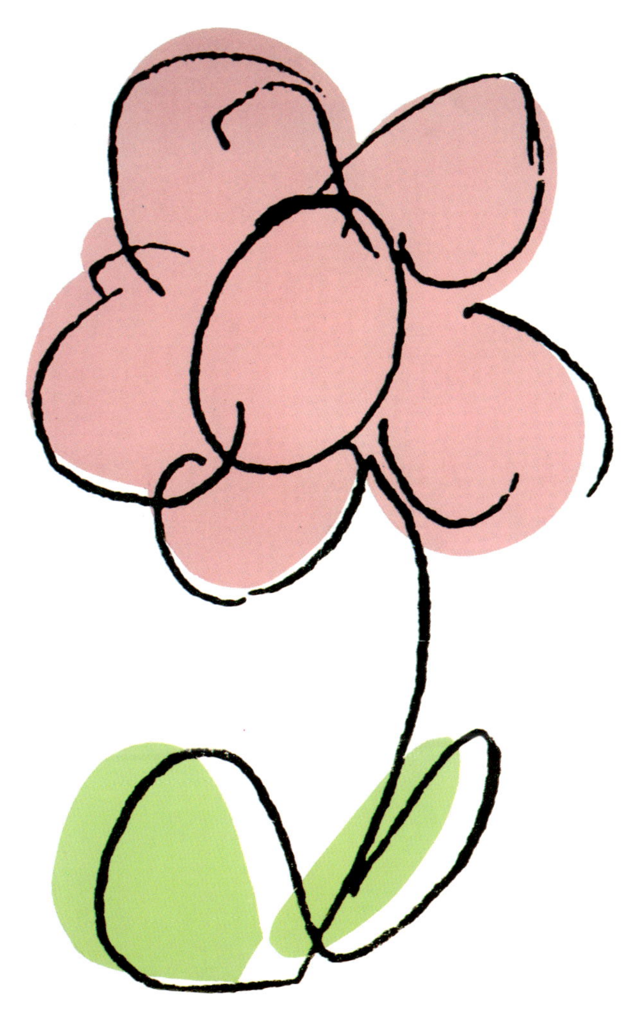

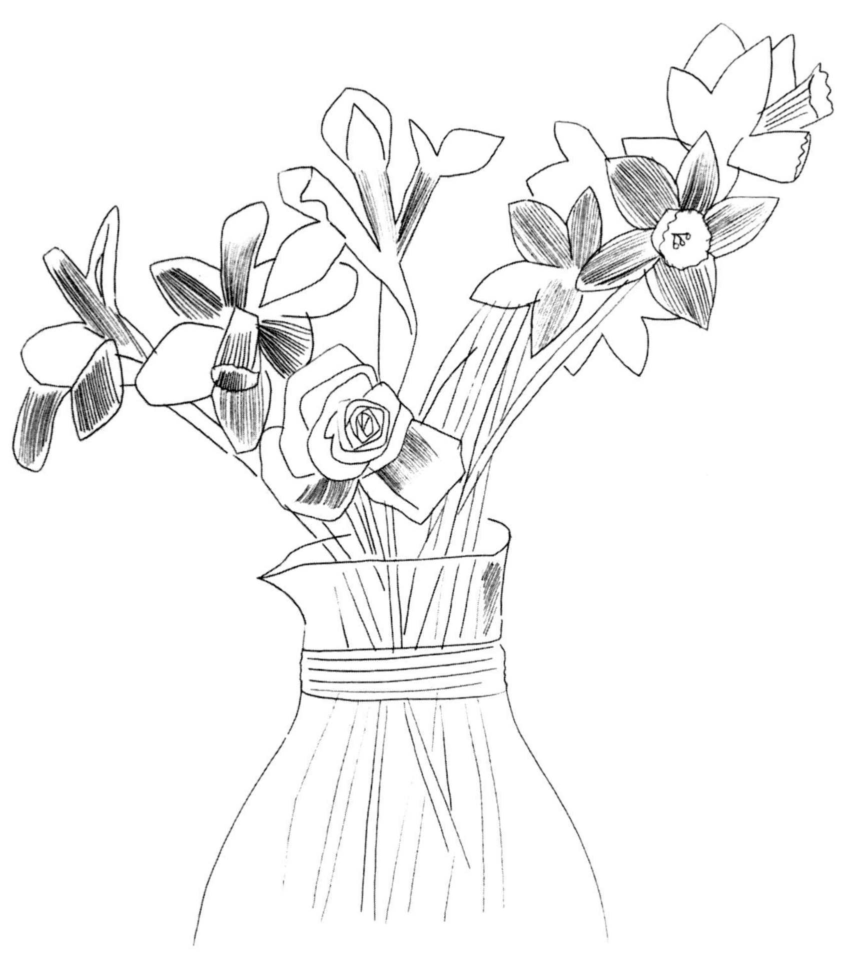

There were **white orchids**

on the

girls'

plates.

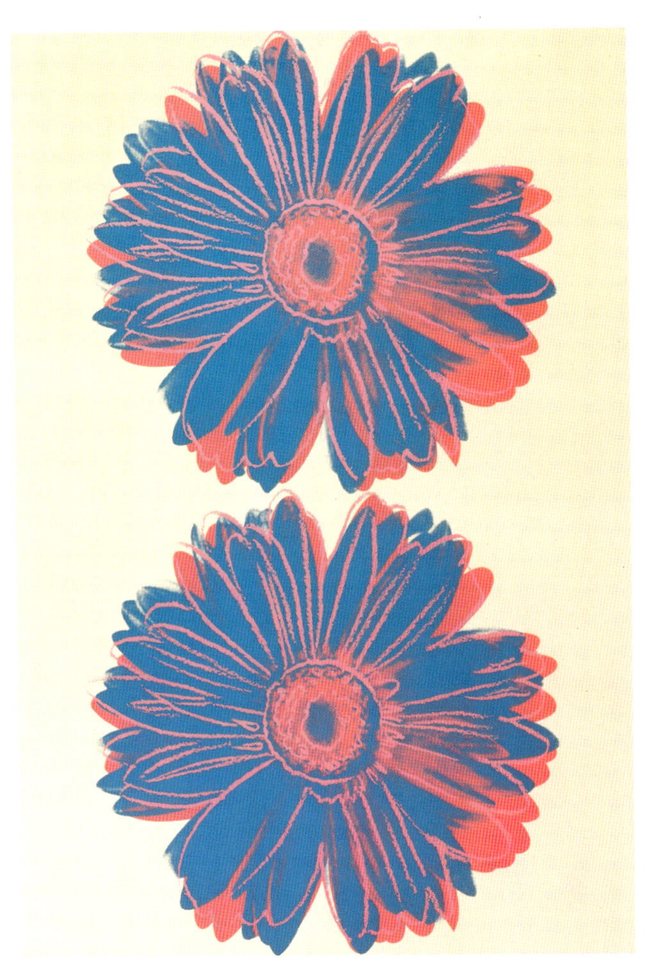

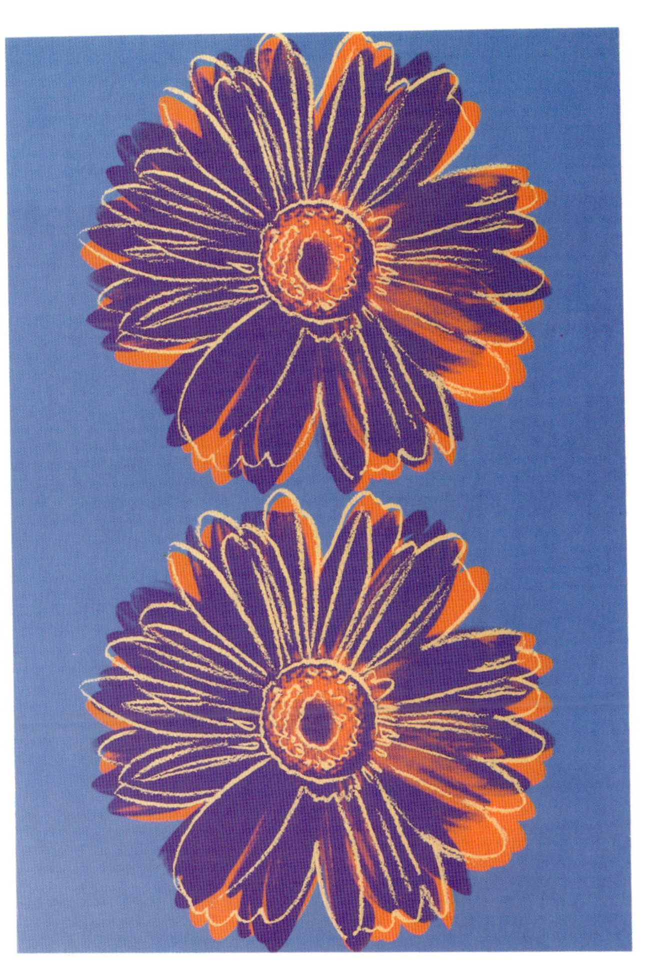

In the city,

even the trees

in the parks

work hard.

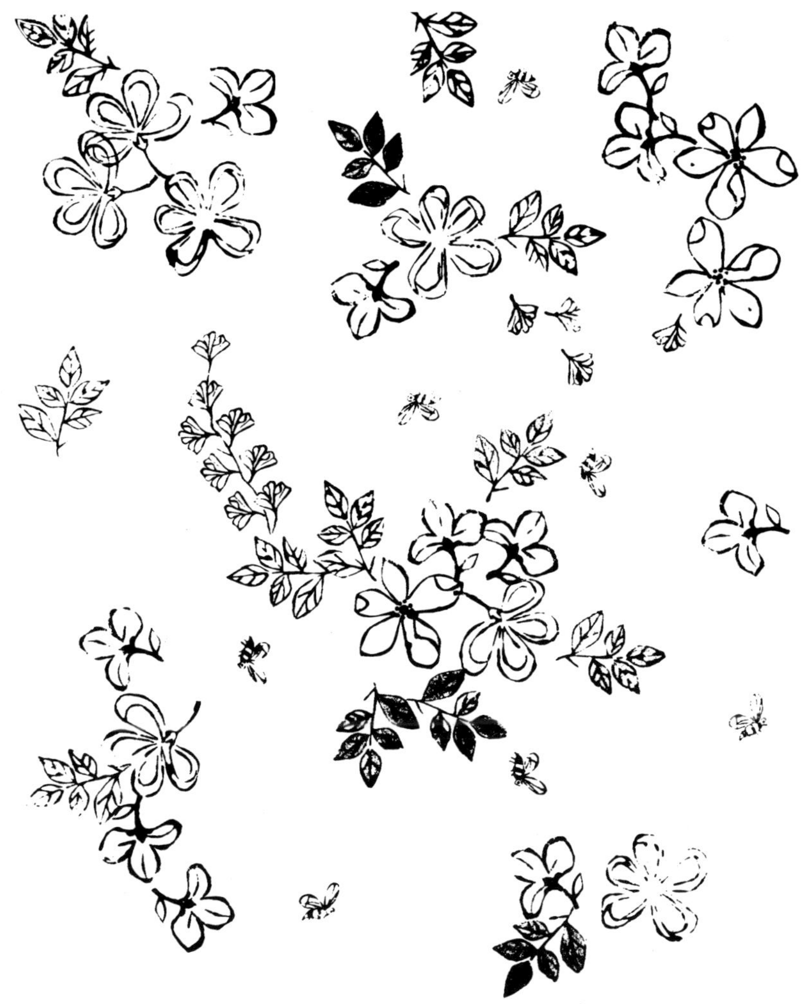

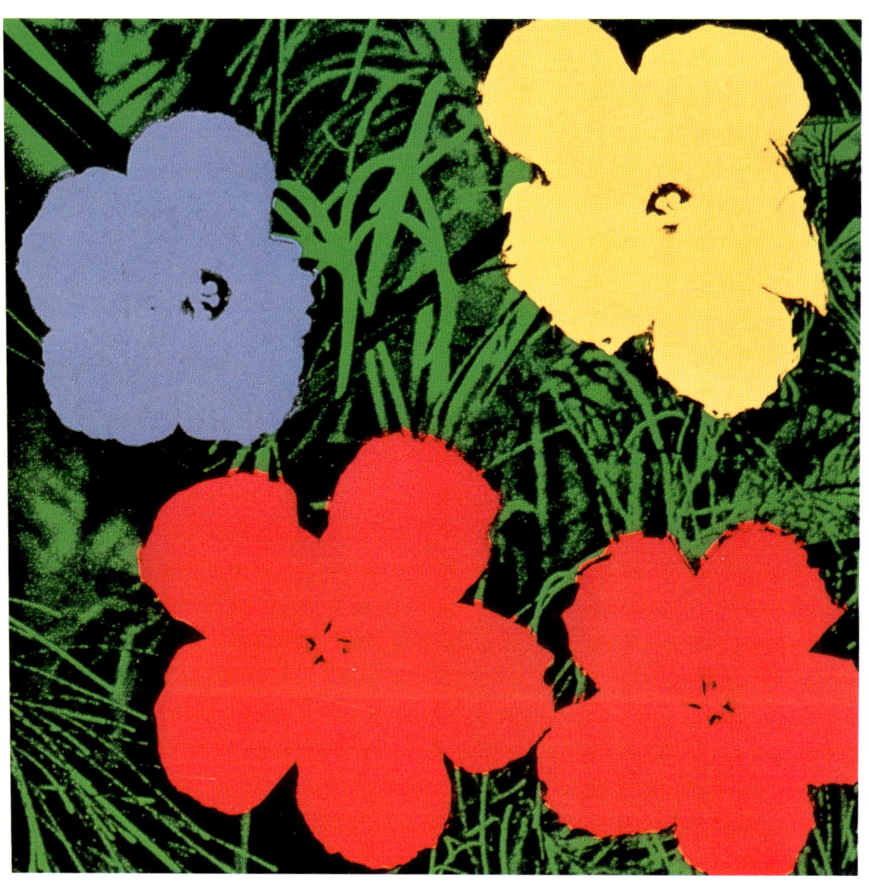

They flew in **violets**

for

the

ladies.

It wasn’t

my night,

it was

their night.

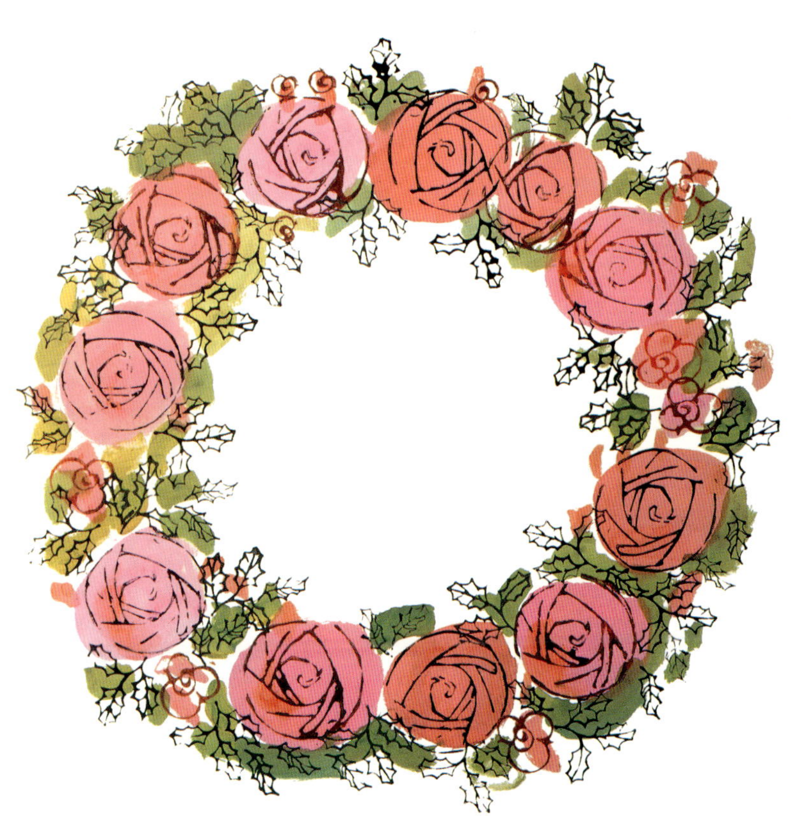

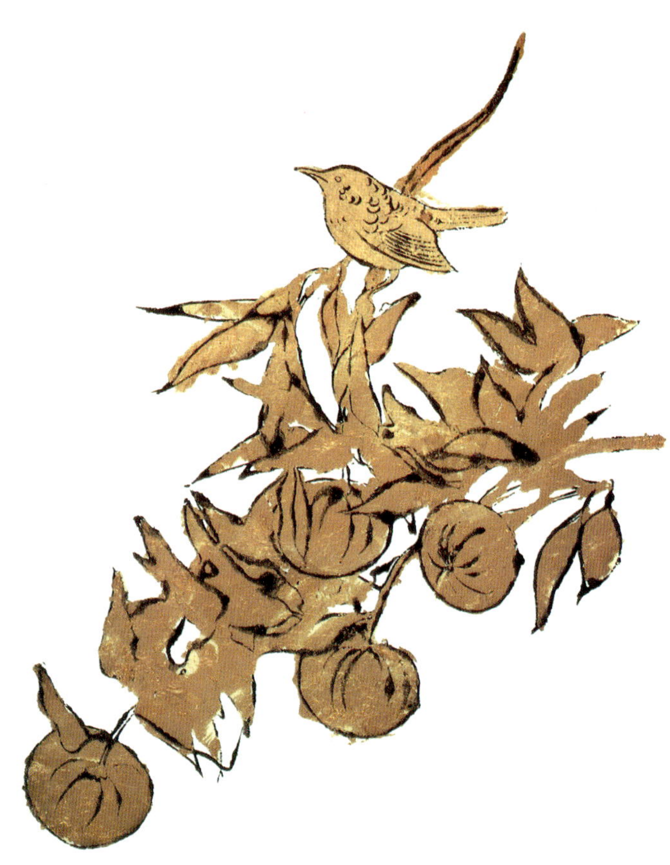

The trees and the grass
all look
great.

I decided
to grow
along the
sidelines,
like a good
wallflower.

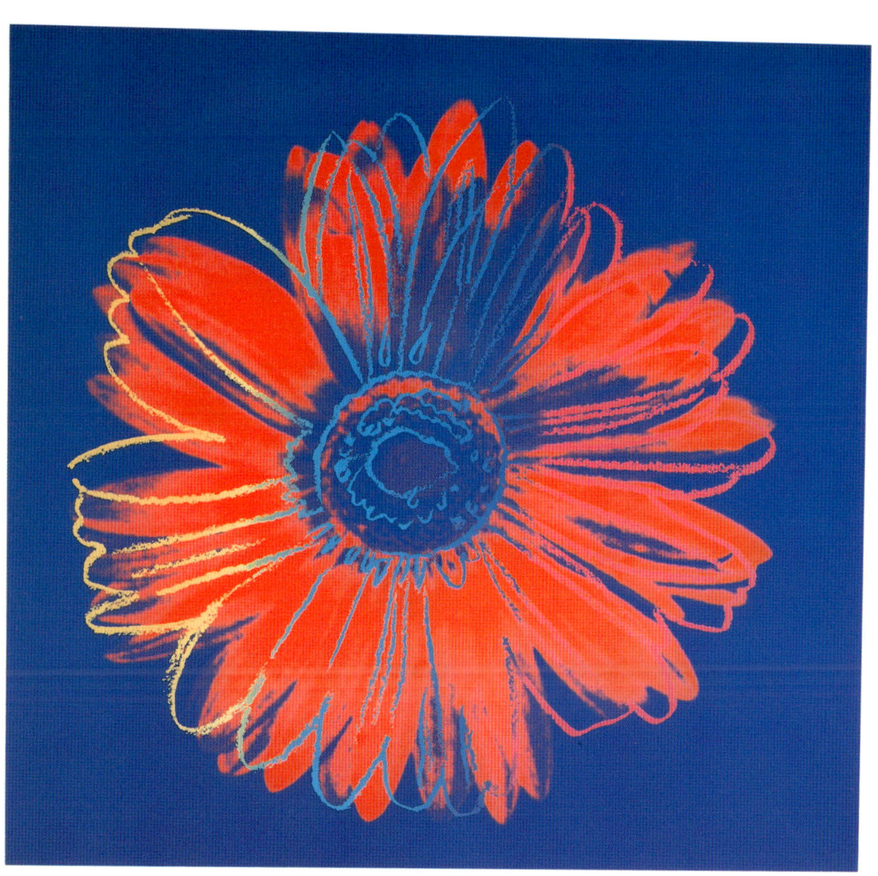

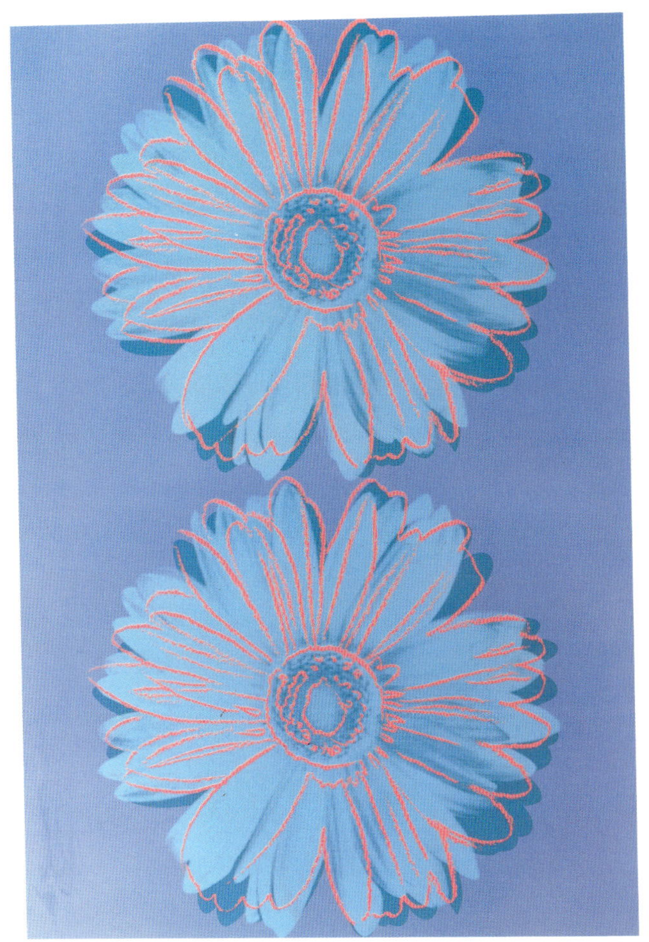

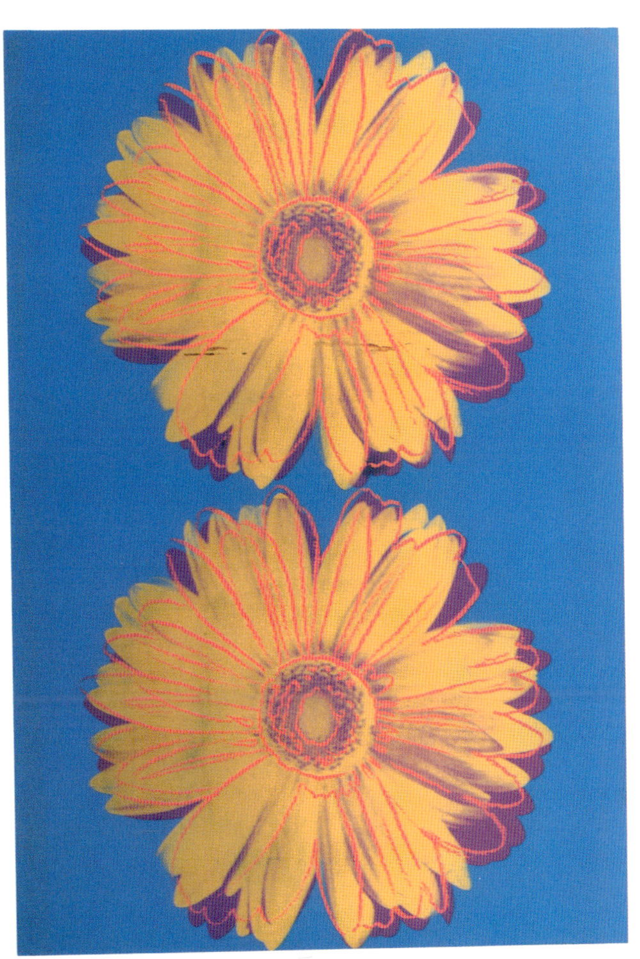

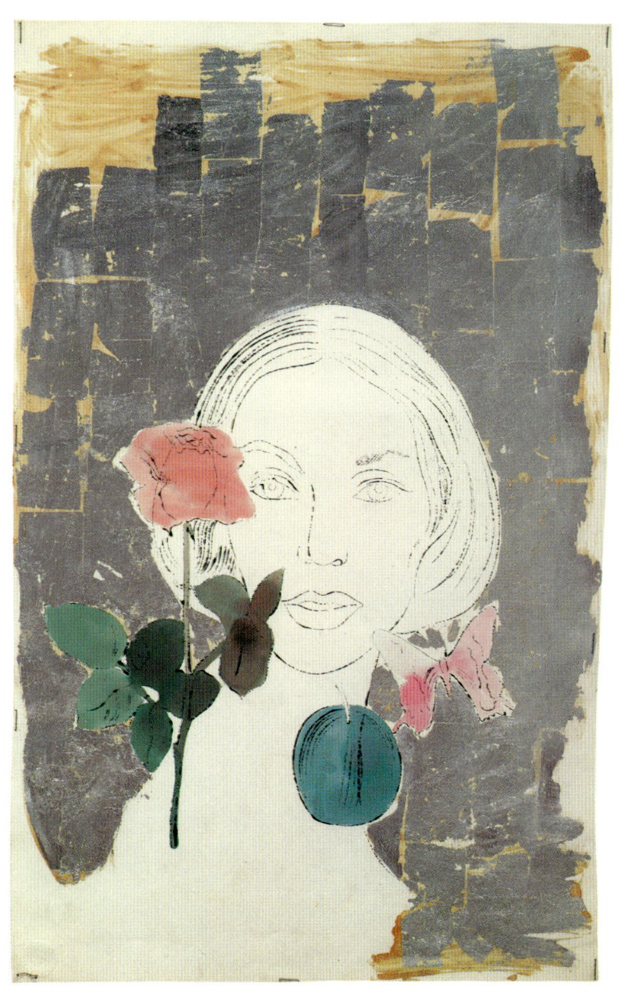

I love

to smell the flowers

but I can't.

He thought

the flowers
had a hard time
at
parties.

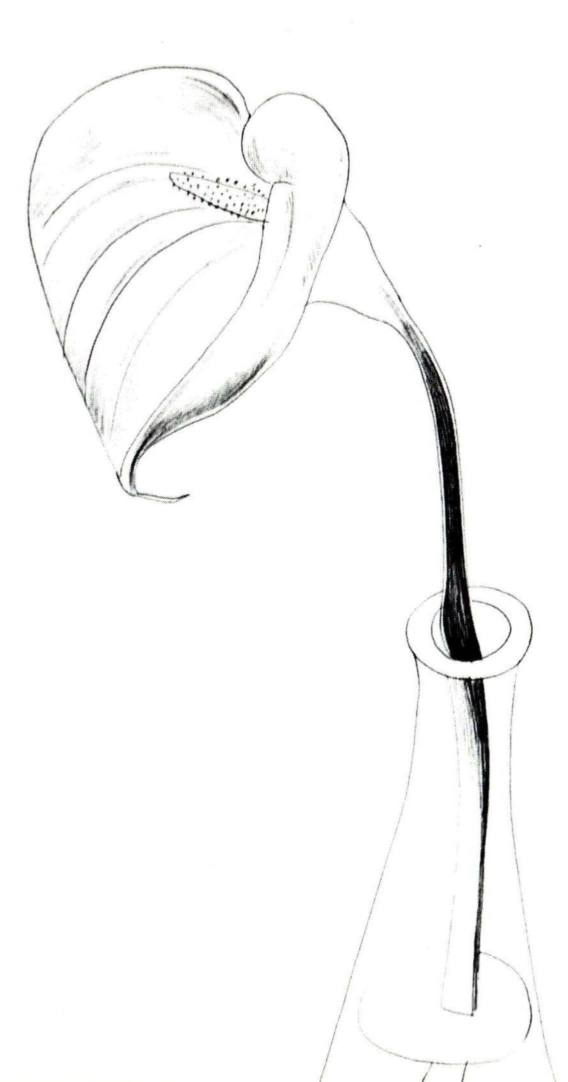

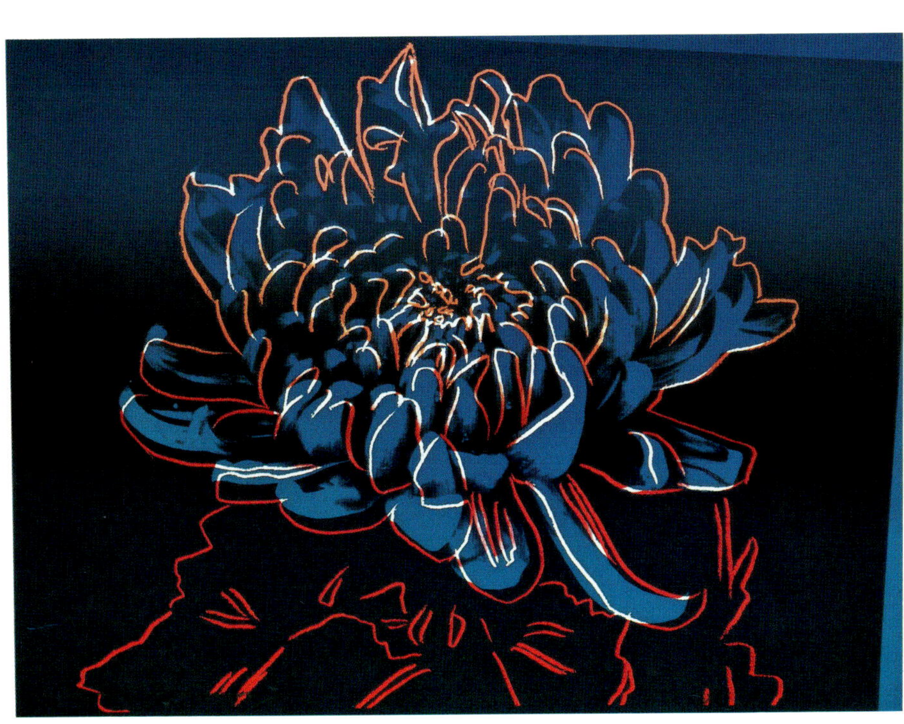

He's very conscious of getting the right *kind* of flowers.

I wondered what

the **stages** were in a

career

as a florist.

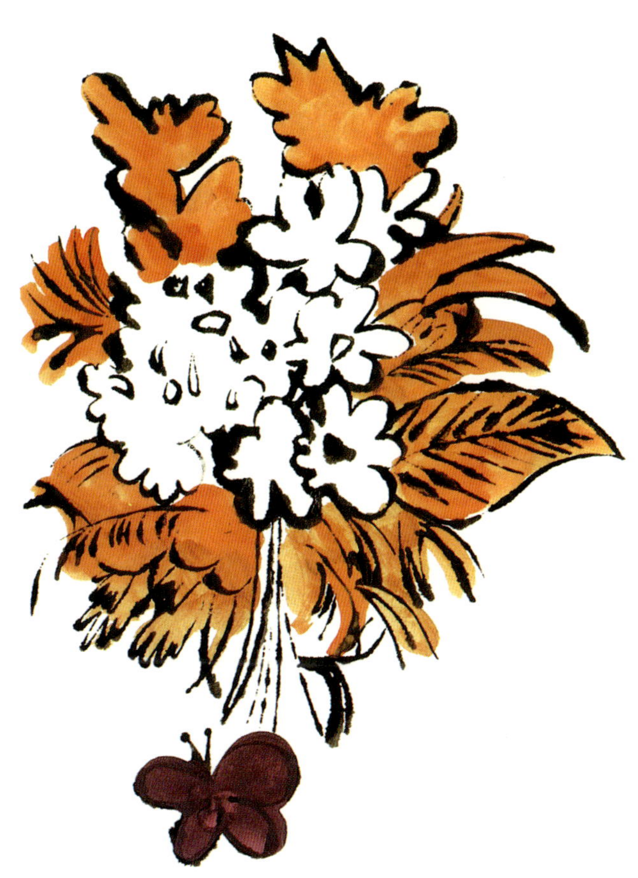

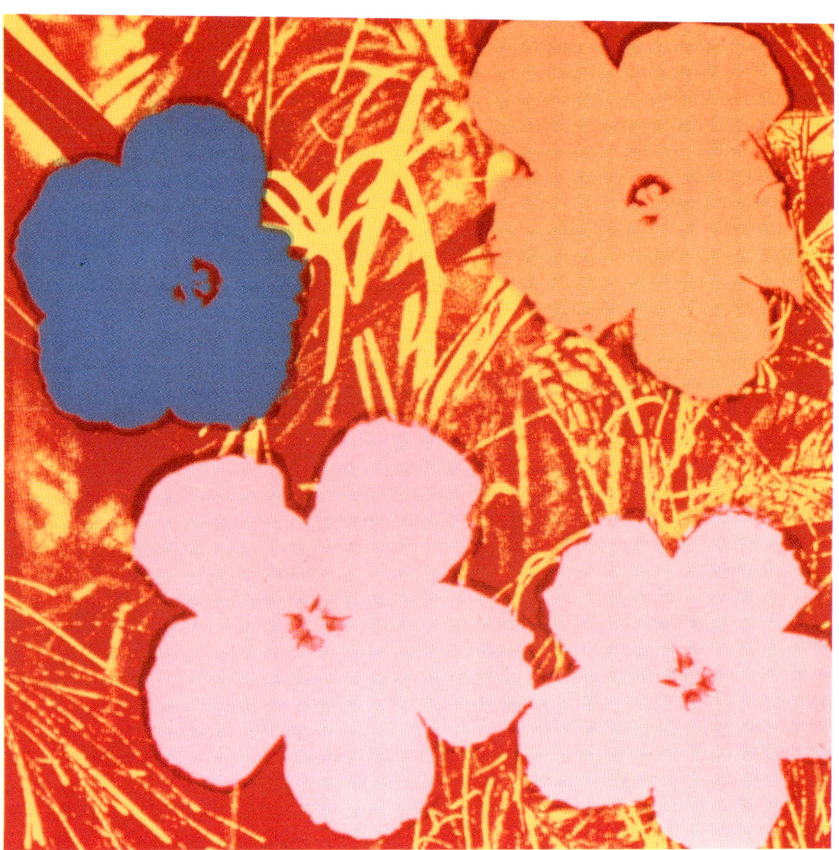

I specifically
chose to exhibit
my flower paintings in France...because I thought
the French would
like flowers,
what with

Renoir

and so on.

One red petunia

in a window box
will look very beautiful
if all the rest of them are
white,

and vice-versa.

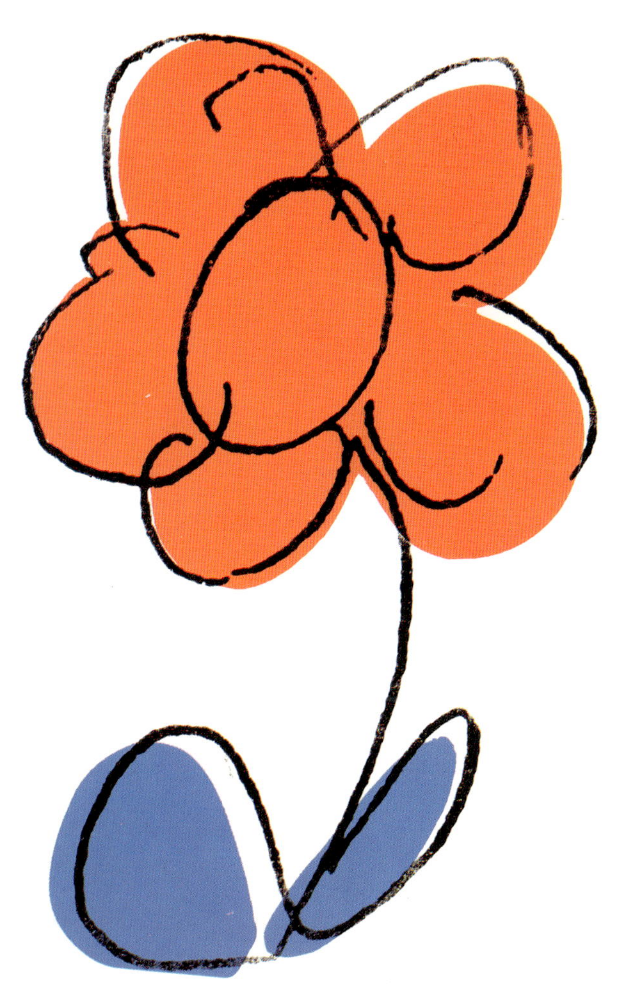

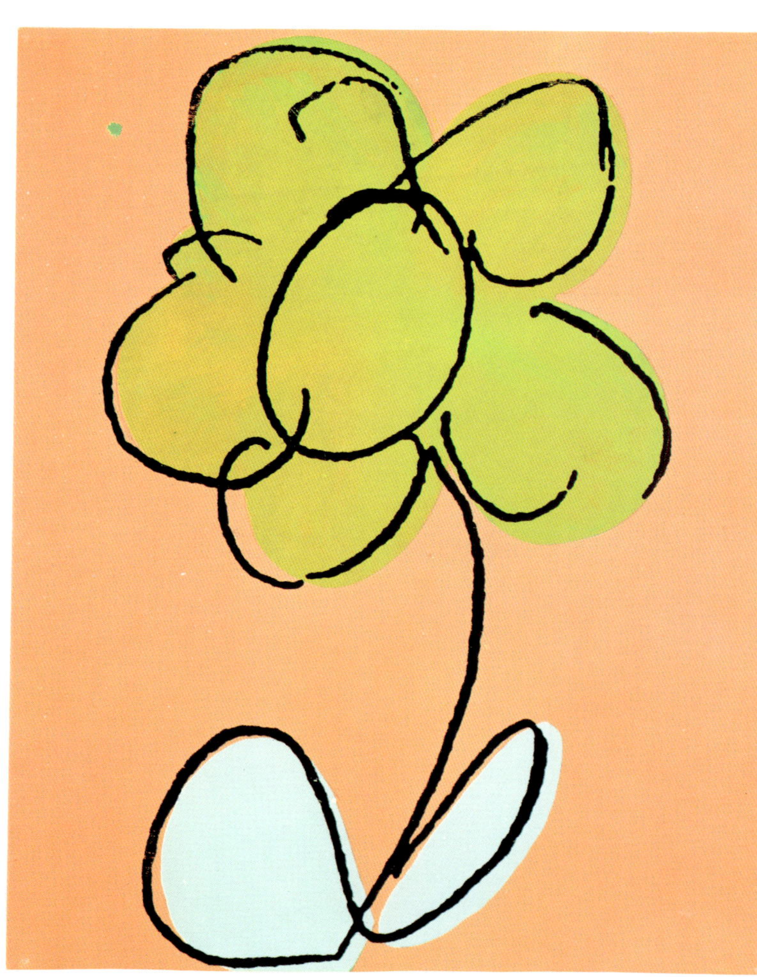

I liked the flowers

because

they looked like

a cheap awning.

They had thousands
of gardenias—

her favorite.

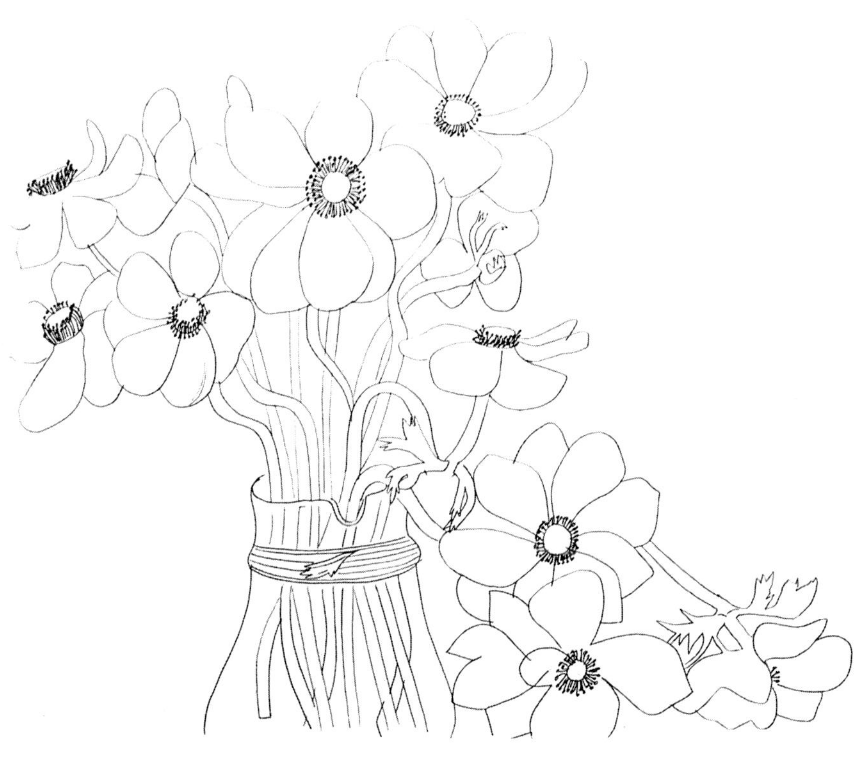

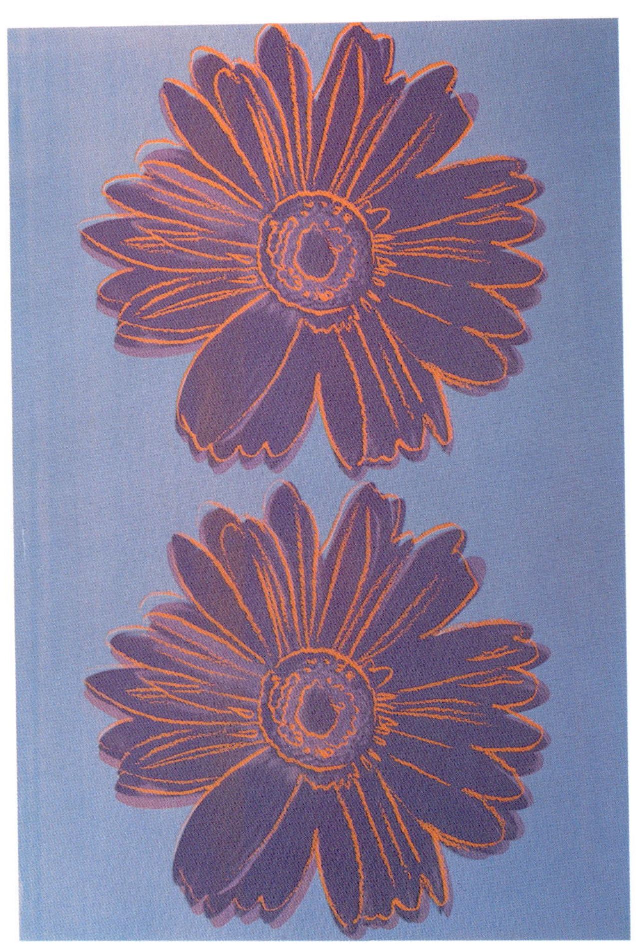

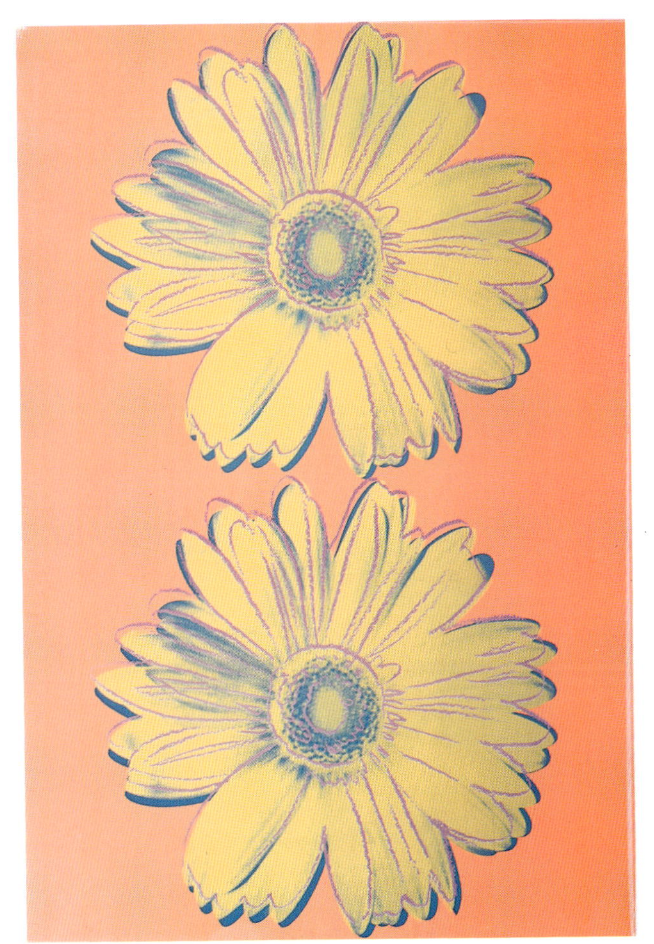

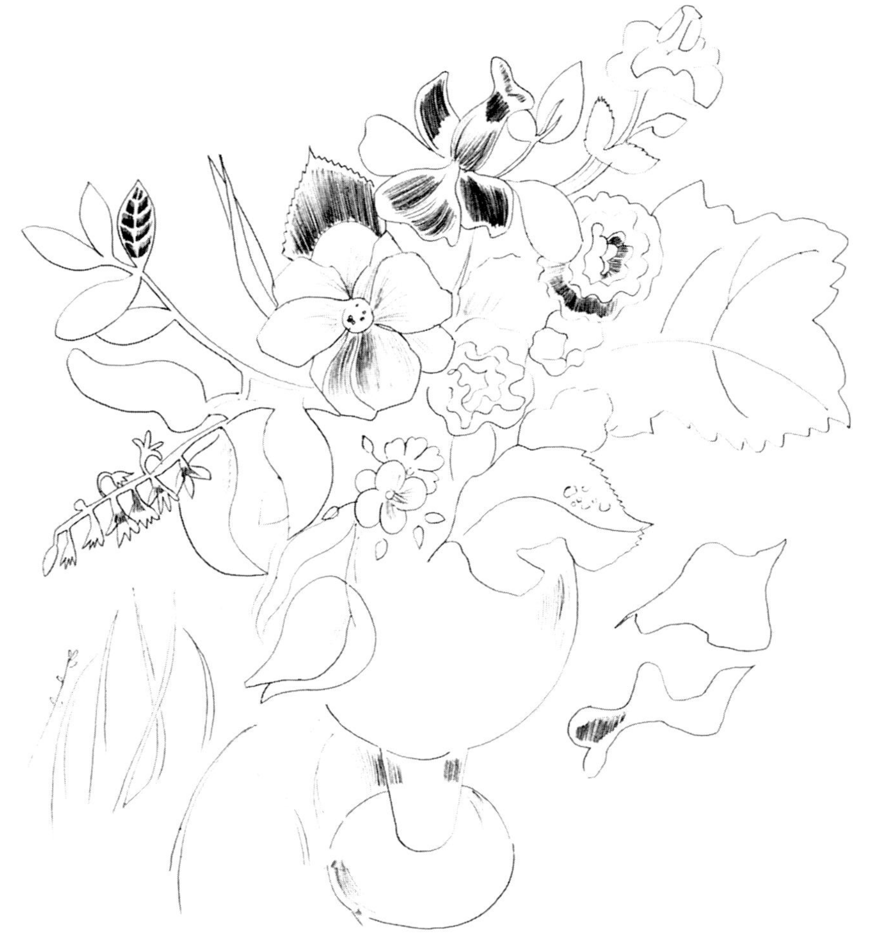

The decorations were
fabulous,

vases as big as people,

filled with flowers.

It **usually** happens

s o s l o w l y

that you
don’t even
notice it.

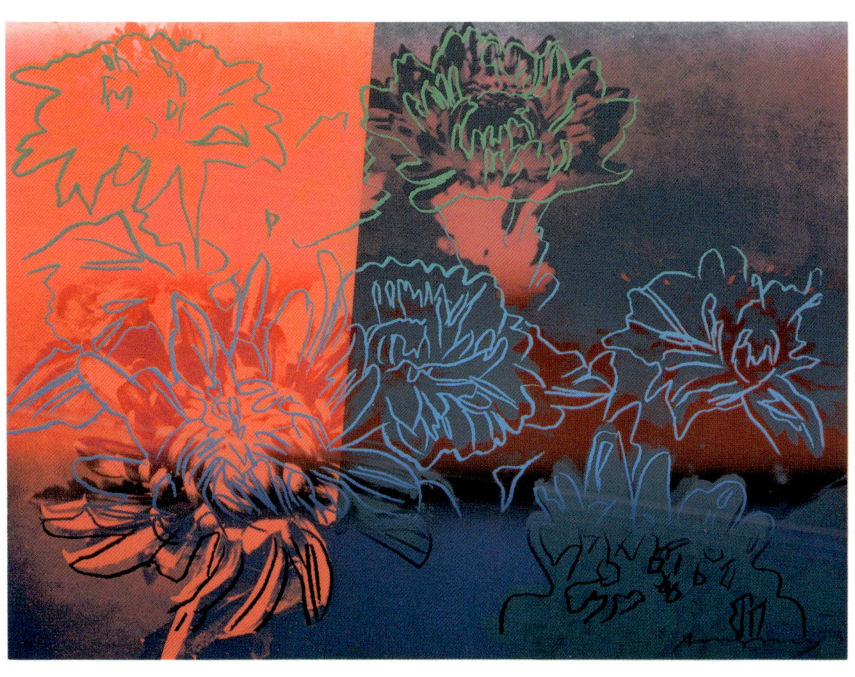

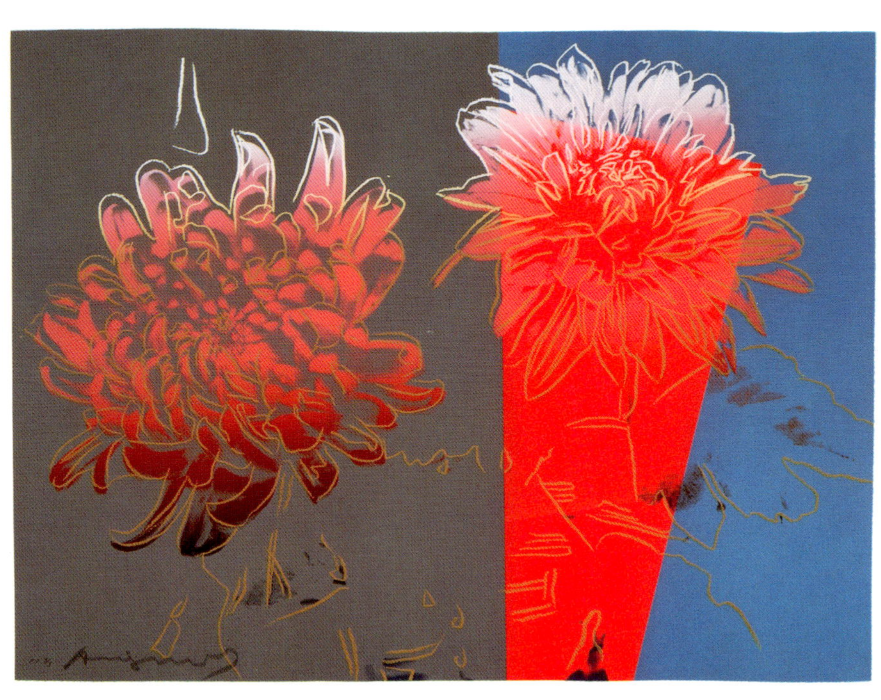

But then

you **watch**

for a while.

When I'm **walking around New York**

I'm always aware of the **smells** around me.

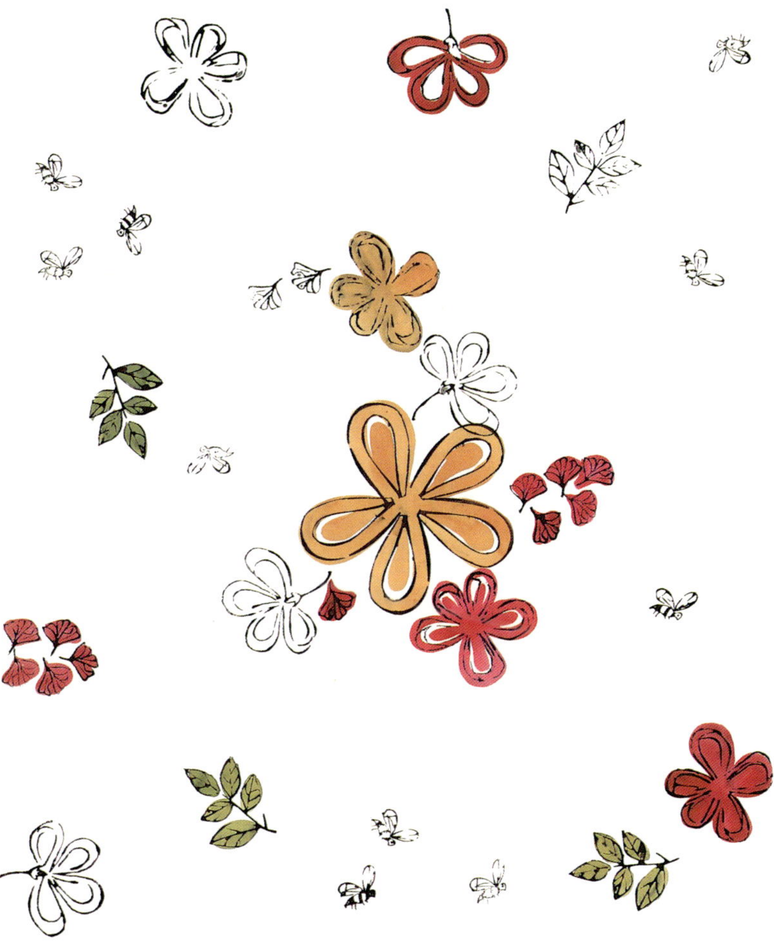

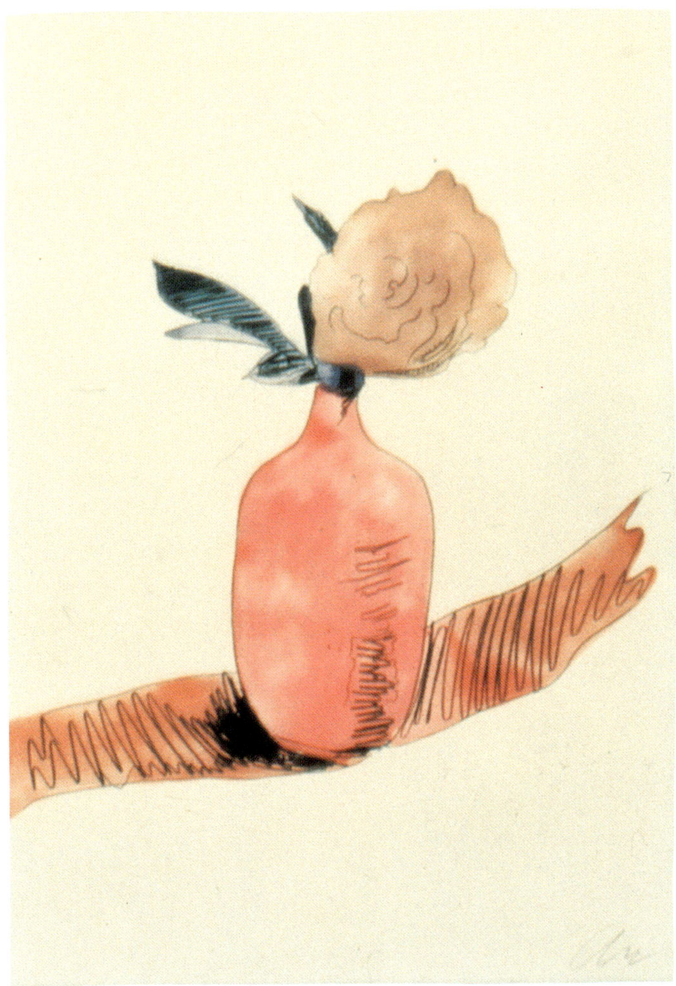

I hate Sundays:

there's nothing open
except plant stores
and bookstores.

Whenever
I smell it
again

it will always remind me
of those three months.

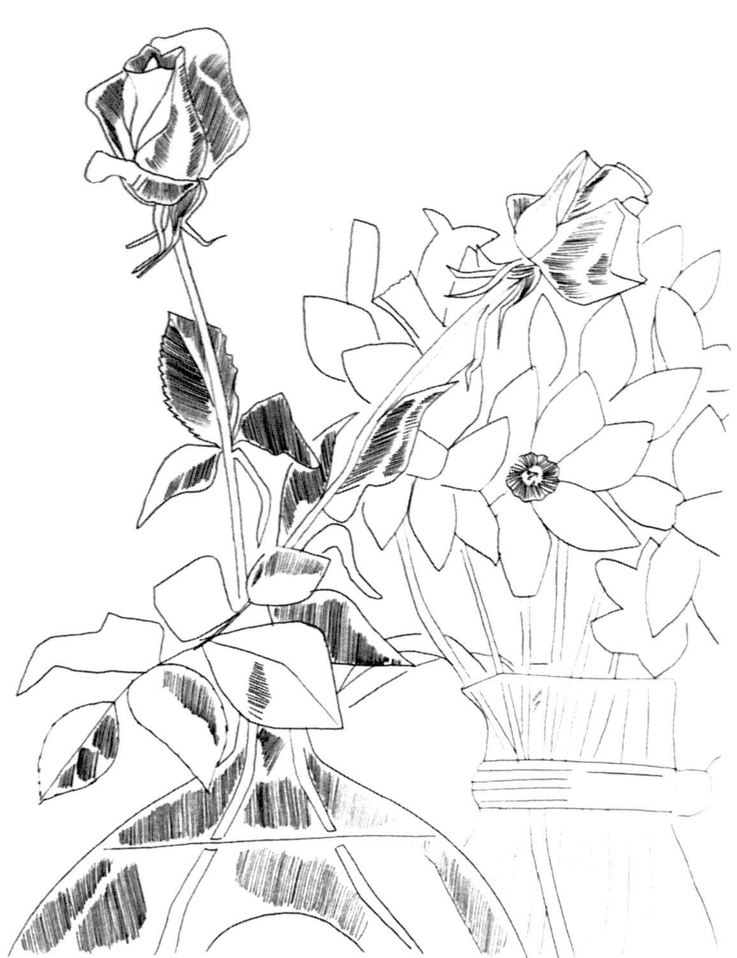

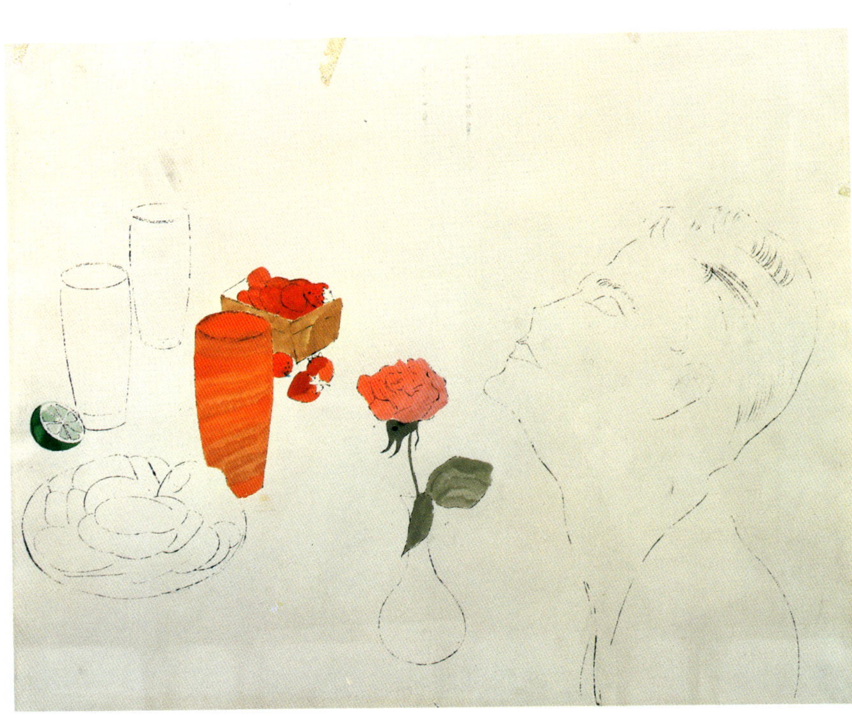

Of the five senses,
smell
has the closest thing
to the full power
of the past.

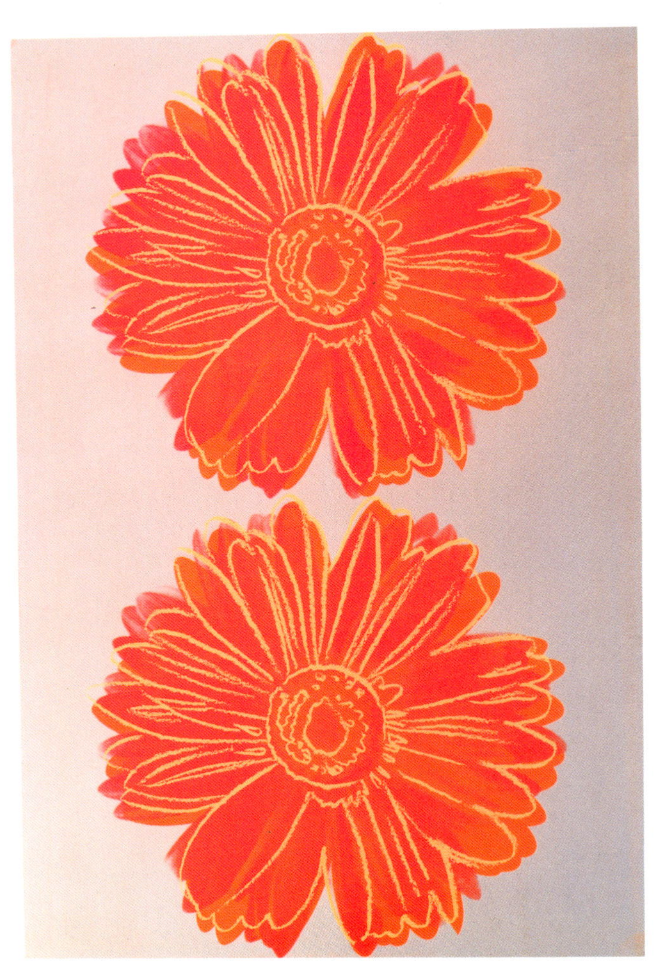

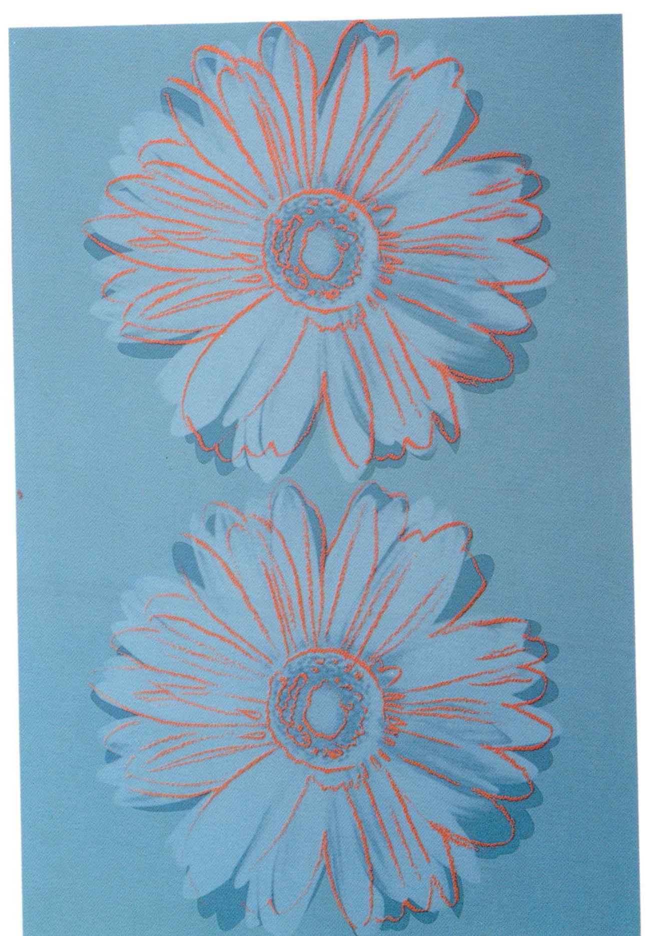

We said our good nights
and thank-yous

and I hope I remember to send flowers.

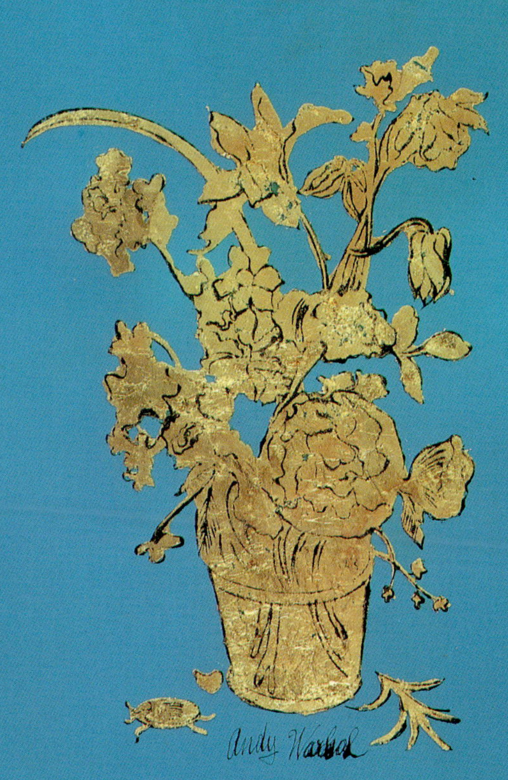
Andy Warhol

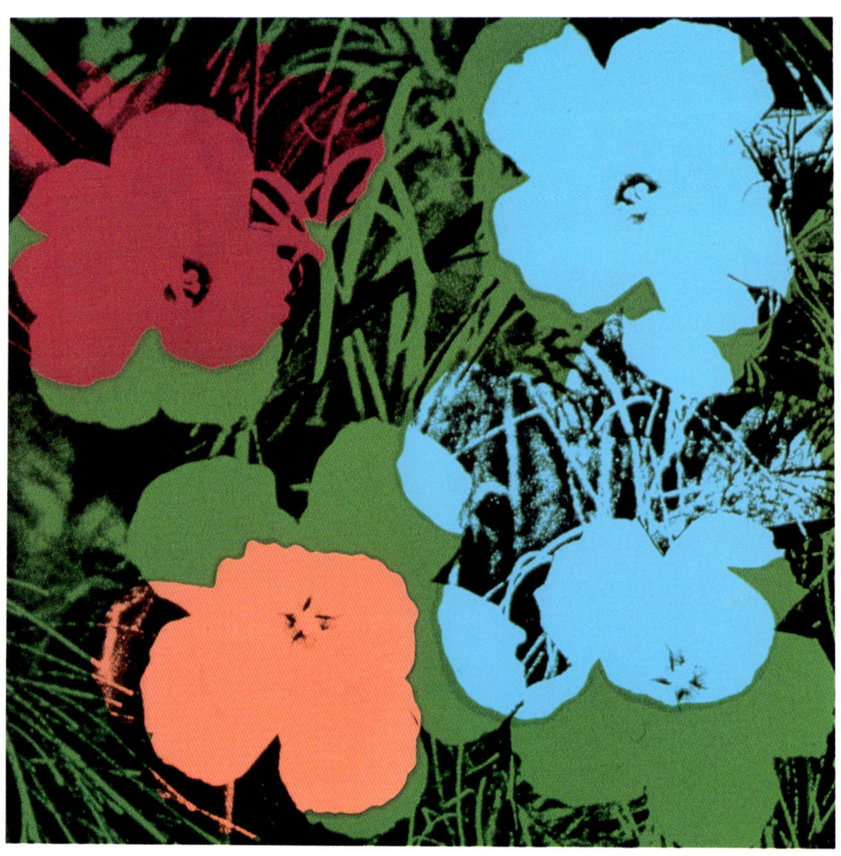

All quotations are by Andy Warhol
and were first published as follows:

Pages 6, 8, 11, 12, 20, 26, 33, 39, 48, 62, 65, 66, 69:
Andy Warhol. *The Philosophy of Andy Warhol (from A to B and Back Again).* New York: Harcourt Brace Jovanovich, 1975.

Pages 58, 61:
Andy Warhol. *America.* New York: Harper & Row, 1985.

Page 34:
Andy Warhol. *POPism: The Warhol '60s.* New York: Harcourt Brace Jovanovich, 1980.

Pages 15, 16, 19, 40, 43, 44, 52:
Andy Warhol and Pat Hackett. *Andy Warhol's Party Book.* New York: Crown Publishers, 1988.

Pages 23, 29, 30, 57, 72:
Pat Hackett, Editor. *The Andy Warhol Diaries.* New York: Warner Books, 1989.

Pages 47, 51:
Mike Wren. *Andy Warhol in His Own Words.* London: Omnibus Press, 1991.

Captions by page number

Cover
Untitled (Daisy), 1982
Screenprint on two-ply Lenox Museum Board
38" x 38"

Endpapers
Untitled (Stamped Flowers with Curved Stems), c. 1960
Ink on ivory paper
18" x 11 7/8"

3 *Flowers*, 1970
Screenprint on white paper
36" x 36"

5 *Untitled (Still Life: Flowers)*, c. 1956
Ballpoint ink on manila paper
16 3/4" x 13 7/8"

7 *Daisy*, 1982
Screenprint on 2-ply Lenox Museum Board
40" x 60"

9 *Untitled (Still Life: Flowers)*, c. 1956
Ballpoint ink on manila paper
16 3/4" x 13 7/8"

10 *Flower for Dome*, 1982
Screenprint on 2-ply Lenox Museum Board
40" x 60"

13 *Untitled (Hand with Purple Flowers)*, c. 1957
Hand-colored offset print

14 *Untitled (Daisy)*, 1982
Screenprint on two-ply Lenox Museum Board
38" x 38"

17 *Flowers*, 1970
Screenprint on white paper
36" x 36"

18 *Flower*, 1986
Synthetic polymer paint and silkscreen ink on canvas
20" x 16"

21 *Flower*, 1986
Synthetic polymer paint and silkscreen ink on canvas
20" x 16"

22 *Untitled (Still Life: Flowers)*, c. 1956
Ballpoint ink on manila paper
16 3/4" x 13 3/4"

24 *Daisy*, 1982
Screenprint on 2-ply Lenox Museum Board
40 1/8" x 60"

25 *Daisy*, 1982
Screenprint on 2-ply Lenox Museum Board
40" x 60"

27 *Untitled (Stamped Flowers)*, c. 1961
Ink and tempera on Strathmore paper
29" x 23"

28 *Flowers*, 1970
Screenprint on white paper
36" x 36"

31 *Untitled (Christmas Wreath)*, c. 1958
Ink, ink wash, and tempera on Strathmore paper
23" x 24 1/8"

32 *Untitled (Bird on Branch with Leaves and Berries)*, c. 1957
Gold leaf and ink on Strathmore paper
23" x 14 3/8"

35 *Daisy*, 1982
Screenprint on 2-ply Lenox Museum Board
38" x 38"

36 *Daisy*, 1982
Screenprint on 2-ply Lenox Museum Board
40" x 60"

37 *Daisy*, 1982
Screenprint on 2-ply Lenox Museum Board
40 1/8" x 60 1/8"

38 *Untitled (Unknown Female)*, c. 1957
Silver leaf, ink, and ink wash on Strathmore paper
25 1/8" x 16 3/8"

41 *Untitled (Still Life: Flowers)*, c. 1956
Ballpoint ink on manila paper
16 3/4" x 13 3/4"

42 *Kiku*, 1983
One from portfolio of three screenprints printed on Rives BFK
19 5/8" x 26"

45 *Untitled (Still Life: Flowers)*, c. 1956
Ink and ink wash on Strathmore paper
22 7/8" x 13 1/4"

46 *Flowers*, 1970
Screenprint on white paper
36" x 36"

49 *Flower*, 1986
Synthetic polymer paint and silkscreen ink on canvas
20" x 16"

50 *Flower*, 1986
Synthetic polymer paint and silkscreen ink on canvas
20" x 16"

53 *Untitled (Still Life: Flowers)*, c. 1956
Ballpoint ink on manila paper
13 3/4" x 16 3/4"

54 *Daisy*, 1982
Screenprint on 2-ply Lenox Museum Board
40 1/8" x 60"

55 *Daisy*, 1982
Screenprint on 2-ply Lenox Museum Board
40" x 60"

56 *Untitled (Still Life: Flowers)*, c. 1956
Ballpoint ink on manila paper
16 3/4" x 13 7/8"

59 *Kiku*, 1983
One from portfolio of three screenprints printed on Rives BFK
19 5/8" x 26"

60 *Kiku*, 1983
One from portfolio of three screenprints printed on Rives BFK
19 5/8" x 26"

63 *Untitled (Stamped Flowers and Bees)*, c. 1957
Ink and tempera on Strathmore paper
29" x 23"

64 *Flowers (Hand-Colored)*, 1974
One from portfolio of 10 hand-colored screenprints printed on Arches
40 7/8" x 27 1/4"

67 *Untitled (Still Life: Flowers)*, c. 1956
Ballpoint ink on manila paper
16 3/4" x 13 3/4"

68 *Untitled (Tom Royal)*, c. 1952
Ink and ink wash on Strathmore paper
23" x 29"

70 *Daisy*, 1982
Screenprint on two-ply Lenox Museum Board
40 1/8" x 60 1/8"

71 *Daisy*, 1982
Screenprint on two-ply Lenox Museum Board
40" x 60"

73 *Untitled (Flower Arrangement)*, c. 1956
Gold leaf and ink on colored graphic art paper
16" x 12"

74 *Flowers*, 1970
Screenprint on white paper
36" x 36"

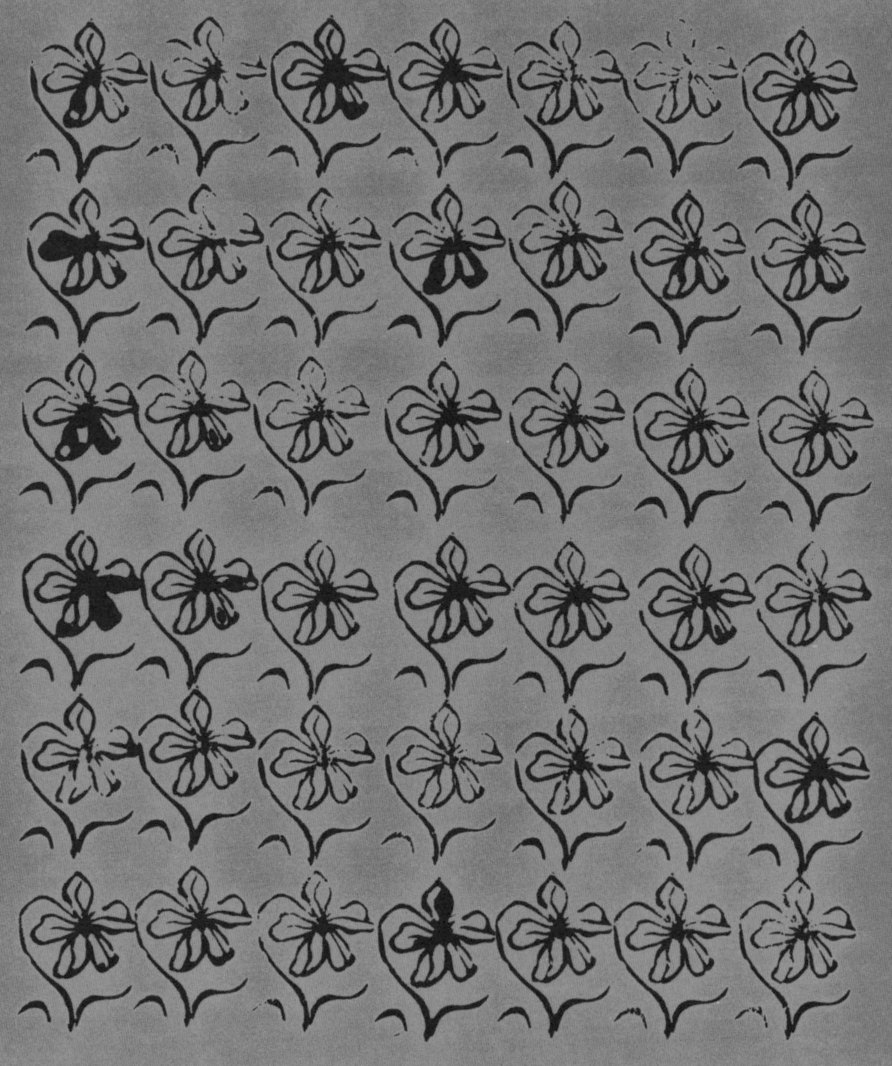